15 GREEK MYTH MINI-BOOKS

by Danielle Blood

S·C·H·O·L·A·S·T·I·C
PROFESSIONAL BOOKS

New York ❧ Toronto ❧ London ❧ Auckland ❧ Sydney ❧ Mexico City ❧ New Delhi ❧ Hong Kong ❧ Buenos Aires

For Mom, Dad, and Laura—
with love and gratitude.

Acknowledgments

Special thanks to the following people:

Sarah Longhi, for editing this book so thoughtfully.

Josué Castilleja and Ellen Matlach Hassell,
for designing the elegant cover and interior.

Margeaux Lucas, for beautifully illustrating these stories.

Terry Cooper and Virginia Dooley, for supporting this project.

Betsy Yarbrough, Patricia Kenan-Herrmann,
Kathy Pounds, Elizabeth Aldridge, and Julia Sneden, for
generously sharing their teaching expertise and ideas with me.

Author's Note

Many versions of the Greek myths exist as a result of their being
retold through the centuries. The stories in this book are generally
consistent with popular versions for this age group; however, they
have been adapted to fit the mini-book format and differ in parts
from other retellings. For example, the ending of "Curiosity and the
Box" offers a nontraditional interpretation of how hope survives.

Cover design by Josué Castilleja

Cover and interior illustrations by Margeaux Lucas

Interior design by Ellen Matlach Hassell
for Boultinghouse & Boultinghouse

ISBN: 0-439-21561-7

❧ CONTENTS ❧

Greek Myth Mini-Books

INTRODUCTION

"I thought the Greek myths were going to be boring!" one of my students said midway through our mythology unit.

"Why did you think that?" I asked.

"Because they're so old!"

Greek mythology was one of my favorite units to teach because students were always so surprised that these ancient stories could relate to today's world—and, most important, to their own lives. The themes are timeless: love, courage, power, ambition, loss, jealousy, fear, triumph, and much more. The characters show both heroic qualities and common flaws. They experience both success and failure. Even the Greek gods and goddesses are far from perfect. They become angry, they hold grudges, and they even fall in love.

The myths served many purposes in ancient times. Some of them explained natural phenomena, such as the rising and setting sun or the changing seasons. The myths also explored philosophical issues that people continue to grapple with today. Although these stories are entertaining and fanciful, they deal with issues of real life—and real life does not always have a neat, happy ending. This is one of the most intriguing aspects of mythology, especially since young readers have come to expect stories to end happily. A sad ending can be baffling to students, but it can also lead them think about the stories on a deeper level. It motivates them to ask questions, search for answers, discuss ideas, and make connections to their own experiences.

Once students are familiar with these stories, they will begin to find references to Greek mythology all around them. Museums are filled with paintings and sculptures depicting the gods and goddesses. Students can even find mythology in the Yellow Pages! When students have read about Hermes, a logo of a winged sandal takes on new meaning. After they've learned about gold-loving King Midas, they'll understand expressions like "the Midas touch."

Students will make connections as they learn vocabulary words, such as *narcissistic*, *arachnid*, and *titanic*. Mythology also provides young readers with an excellent foundation for their future studies, as it is the basis for so many important pieces of literature.

These mini-books are short retellings of 15 favorite myths, featuring simple text, lively illustrations, and speech balloons. The comic-strip style and mini-book format help make the stories accessible and inviting to students of all reading levels. For quick reference, you'll find a glossary and pronunciation guide at the back of the book. To extend learning, suggested activities for each mini-book are provided on pages 6–9. There are a number of ways you can incorporate the mini-books into your studies. Here are some suggestions:

- Enhance language arts or social studies units on ancient Greece.
- Supplement classroom texts.
- Motivate reluctant readers.
- Support visual learners.
- Introduce myths in a quick, simple way.
- Review myths at the end of the unit.
- Prompt a class discussion.
- Introduce a writing assignment.
- Provide students with take-home materials.

Students sometimes underestimate how much they'll enjoy a reading experience, especially if the material is "ancient." These mini-books are one way to help children have fun as they read—and encourage them to become fans of Greek mythology!

HOW TO USE THIS BOOK

Passed down through the centuries, first orally and later in writing, the Greek myths have evolved into many different versions. These 15 mini-books are short retellings of favorite myths, including the stories of Arachne, Pandora, Daedalus, Atalanta, Perseus, Odysseus, and more. With engaging text, lively illustrations, and a comic-book style, the mini-books appeal to students of all reading levels. The speech balloons and illustrations help readers identify and distinguish among characters, whose names are often difficult to read and remember.

To introduce each mini-book, first review with students the characters who appear in it. On page 79, you will find a glossary and pronunciation guide for the names of all the characters included in this book. Write the characters' names on the board, along with brief information about each one, and review the pronunciations with students. Then give each student photocopied pages of the mini-book and demonstrate the simple assembly steps at right. With guidance, students will be able to assemble their own books without difficulty.

You can use the mini-books in a number of ways. They can be enjoyed on their own or used to supplement other texts. As an inviting introduction, have students read the mini-book before reading a longer version of the myth. Reading the mini-book first allows students to become familiar with the characters and story; this is especially helpful for readers who may struggle with longer, more complicated text. The mini-books can also serve as a fun way to review the myths at the end of a unit.

Students will enjoy reading these mini-books aloud in class. They can play the roles of different characters by reading aloud the text in the speech balloons. The mini-books are also suitable for a short reading assignment at home—and students will be glad to add something light to their backpacks!

Greek mythology is a wonderful springboard for all kinds of activities: small- and large-group discussions, creative writing, short essays, art projects, classroom plays, and much more. Every student and class responds differently to the myths. It is a good idea to generate activities and assignments based on children's reactions and interests. The questions that students raise in class often make excellent topics for writing assignments and other projects. You'll find suggested extension activities and vocabulary words for each mini-book on pages 6–9.

How to Make the Mini-Books

1. Make double-sided copies of the mini-book pages. (Carefully tear along the perforation to remove the pages from the book.) Most mini-books have 8 pages; some have 12 or 16 pages.

    Note: If your machine does not have a double-sided function, first make copies of mini-book pages 1/3. Place these copies in the paper tray with the blank side facing up. Next, make a copy of mini-book pages 2/4 so that page 2/4 copies directly behind page 1/3. Make a test copy to be sure the pages are positioned correctly. Repeat these steps with pages 6/8 and 5/7. (If the book has 12 or 16 pages, repeat these steps with pages 9/11 and 10/12, and 13/15 and 14/16.)

2. Cut apart the mini-book pages along the solid line.

3. Place the pages in numerical order and then staple them along the mini-book's spine.

4. Invite students to color the illustrations.

EXTENSION ACTIVITIES

WELCOME TO MOUNT OLYMPUS

An Introduction to the Greek Gods and Goddesses

This mini-book introduces students to the domains of the gods and goddesses. For example, Poseidon's domain is the sea and Aphrodite's domain is love. Invite students to draw a family tree of the gods and goddesses. Have them write the characters' domains beneath their names and draw pictures representing those domains. These posters can serve as useful study guides and are especially helpful for visual learners. To reinforce the concept of domain, invite students to draw a picture of their own "domains." For example, a student might write that her domain is the soccer field. Students can also decide on the domains of family members, friends, and celebrities.

VOCABULARY: lofty, deities, overthrow, nectar, yearned, potion, domain, divine

JOURNEY TO THE UNDERWORLD

The Story of Persephone and Demeter

Ask students to imagine that they are Persephone trapped in the Underworld. Invite them to write several entries in her diary describing her observations of the Underworld, her feelings about being kidnapped, and her feelings toward Hades. What does she miss about the world above? Does she have a plan to escape? How does she feel about Zeus's decision to make her spend half the year in the Underworld and half the year on Earth? Encourage students to add illustrations to their diary entries.

VOCABULARY: whims, embedded, descended, grieved, barren, pomegranate

A TALE OF TWO SPINNERS

The Story of Arachne and Athena

Instead of insulting the goddess of wisdom, Arachne could have learned from Athena. Explain to students what an apprentice is. Ask them to imagine that they are applying to be an apprentice to one of the Greek gods. Have them write a business letter applying for a job. Which god or goddess would they want to work for? What might the job entail? If a student loves to swim or sail, he or she might write to Poseidon. If a student loves to travel, a job with Hermes would be ideal. Encourage them to use persuasive writing to convince the god or goddess that they are right for the job.

VOCABULARY: loom, swooped, boastful, mortals, deceitful, scurried

CURIOSITY AND THE BOX

The Story of Pandora

The end of this myth is one of the most memorable moments in Greek mythology: Pandora opens the forbidden box and all the evils escape to plague humankind. Students might enjoy a lighthearted activity after reading this serious ending. Ask students to think of something that they would like trapped in the box where it could not bother them. Encourage them to choose something from their own lives, such as traffic jams, broken VCRs, homework, and so on. Have each student write one or two of these "pesky" things on a small square of paper. Collect the squares in a small box and then open the box and read them aloud to the class. Invite students to imagine and write about the time before Pandora opened the box and let all these pests escape.

VOCABULARY: inlaid, spite, plague, optimistic, temporary

A Trip Around the World
The Story of Phaethon and Apollo

Phaethon and Apollo are the subjects of many pieces of art. Show students paintings and sculptures that depict Phaethon, Apollo, and other characters from Greek mythology. Ask them to identify the characters in each piece of art and describe what is happening in the scene. What symbols help students identify the characters? Which point in the story did the artist choose to show? Why do students think the artist chose this particular moment in the story? Have students choose a myth to illustrate. Ask them to think about the moment in the story that they think is the most interesting and important. Invite them to draw that scene, including as much information as they can about what is happening. Encourage them to include symbols that will help the viewer identify the characters.

VOCABULARY: ordinary, boasting, shielded, eager, veer, bewildered, bolted, plunged, withered, minor

Gossip and Vanity
The Story of Echo and Narcissus

Many Greek myths explain natural phenomena: Apollo's chariot explains how the sun rises and sets; the story of Athena and Arachne explains how spiders became weavers; and the story of Echo and Narcissus explains why there are echoes and narcissus flowers. After reading the story of Echo and Narcissus, students will be inspired to write their own creation myths. Invite them to write a creative story that explains how something in modern-day life came into existence. For example, they can explain why there are televisions, spaceships, or football.

VOCABULARY: eavesdropping, nymph, chatter, prattle, impudent, aimlessly, devastated

Music Makes the Underworld Go 'Round
The Story of Orpheus and Eurydice

In this story, Orpheus travels to the Underworld to find his wife. Longer versions of this myth provide wonderful descriptions of the Underworld and its inhabitants. Share some of these descriptions with students and then invite them to draw, color, and label a map of the Underworld. Have them show Orpheus's path along with the characters he meets on the way: Charon, Cerberus, Tantalus, Sisyphus, Persephone, Hades, and Eurydice. They may need to use several sources, such as the description provided in *Heroes, Gods, and Monsters of the Greek Myths* by Bernard Evslin.

VOCABULARY: lyre, lulled, eternal, doomed, eternity, grasp

Cupid Falls in Love
The Story of Cupid and Psyche

The ending of this myth may perplex students. In other retellings, Cupid eventually forgives Psyche. Invite students to write their own ending. They can either start where the mini-book leaves off, or go back into the story and start from a different point. Does Psyche take her sisters' advice to peek at Cupid while he's sleeping? Does Cupid decide that Psyche deserves a second chance?

VOCABULARY: suitors, devoted, withstand, oracle, gust, whisked, gnawed

An Amazing Battle

The Story of Theseus and the Minotaur

The Minotaur, a creature with a man's body and bull's head, is just one of the many unusual creatures in Greek mythology. There are many other creatures that are combinations of different animals: centaurs are half horse and half man; Pan has characteristics of both a goat and a man; and Pegasus is a beautiful winged horse. Ask students to invent their own mythological creature and draw a picture of it. Encourage them to consider the abilities they would like their creature to have. Can it fly? Speak? Swim? Then have students give their creature a name and write a myth about it. Their myth might explain how their creature came into existence, or it might describe an adventure that the creature has.

VOCABULARY: sacrificed, oppose, devoured, slay, labyrinth, boarding, haste, horizon

Dangerous Heights

The Story of Daedalus and Icarus

Ask students to imagine what life was like in ancient times without the conveniences that we are accustomed to today. Invite them to imagine that they are Daedalus, the clever inventor. What would they invent to make life easier? What materials would they use to build their contraption? Have students draw a picture of their invention and write a brief description of what it does. Encourage them to write their own myth about Daedalus and his latest invention.

VOCABULARY: labyrinth, mercy, dismay, clumps

The Race for Love

The Story of Atalanta

Atalanta holds an unusual competition in this story: a race to win her hand in marriage. Invite students to come up with different kinds of competitions in which mythological characters might compete. Ask students to imagine an Olympics on Mt. Olympus. What events would they include and whom would they choose to compete in each one? This is good way to review the different gods and goddesses. Zeus might hurl thunderbolts, Athena could enter the fencing competition, and Poseidon could go for the gold in surfing. Encourage students to be creative as they invent their own events. Divide the class into small groups. Encourage each group to think of an event, describe the event in a paragraph, and enter five gods or goddesses. Have the groups share their events and then the rest of the class can vote on the winners.

VOCABULARY: fend, panic, ravaging, stingy, cunning, ferocity, pelt, safeguarded, hearth, consumed, suitors, vow, potential, delectable, tunic

The Golden Touch

The Story of King Midas

Midas learns that it is possible to have too much of a good thing. Discuss this idea with students. Can they think of other "good things" that it is possible to have too much of? How about ice cream, video games, or television? Invite students to write their own comic strip about a character who gets too much of a good thing. Does the character learn a lesson, as Midas did? Compile students' comic strips to make a classroom funny pages.

VOCABULARY: satisfy, standard, appetite, glee, quench, pathetic

CARVED TO PERFECTION
The Story of Pygmalion

In this myth, Pygmalion's wish comes true: The statue of his ideal partner comes to life. Ask students to think of an inanimate object that they would like to come to life. It could be anything: a favorite toy, a refrigerator, or even a pair of sneakers. Invite them to write a creative story about this new "being." What is its name? Where does it live? What would a day in the life of this animate object be like? Encourage them to add illustrations.

VOCABULARY: chiseled, solitary, emerge, exhaustion, pedestal, witty, altar, flush, embraced

A PETRIFYING QUEST
The Story of Perseus and Medusa

This myth is filled with symbols, such as Hermes' winged sandals and Medusa's snake-hair. Symbols from Greek mythology are frequently used today. Many companies use names or symbols from mythology to represent their services or products. For example, several companies use Hermes' winged sandal as their logo. Ask students what message this symbol sends to the consumer. Show students several examples of Greek references in modern life and ask them to think about why companies chose to use these names or symbols. You can also challenge students to find several examples of names or symbols from Greek mythology on their own. Or have students make up their own company and use a meaningful symbol from Greek mythology as its logo.

VOCABULARY: consulted, oracles, fate, transformed, suspecting, fend, noble, quest, sickle, territory, petrifying, sacrificed, swooped, destined, halt, souvenir, spectator

THE MYSTERIOUS HORSE
The Story of the Trojan War

Odysseus convinces the Greek soldiers to hide in a giant hollow horse as part of his plan to conquer the Trojans. This clever scheme works in the end, but how do students think the Greek soldiers felt about it beforehand? What might have gone wrong? Ask students to imagine that they are the Greek soldiers hiding inside the horse. What conversation might they have? How do the soldiers feel when the horse is being moved inside the city walls? Invite them to work in small groups to write a short play. Remind them to include Odysseus as one of the characters. The groups can perform their plays for the class.

VOCABULARY: countless, debated, mischievous, surrendered, reveler, rumbling, swift

MYTHOLOGY RESOURCES

BOOKS FOR STUDENTS

Barth, Edna. *Cupid and Psyche: A Love Story*. Boston: Houghton Mifflin, 1976. Grades 4–6.

Colum, Padraic. *Children's Homer: The Adventures of Odysseus and the Tale of Troy*. New York: Macmillan, 1982. Grades 6–8.

D'Aulaires, Ingri and Edgar Parin. *D'Aulaires' Book of Greek Myths*. New York: Doubleday, 1962. Grades 3–6.

Evslin, Bernard. *Heroes, Gods, and Monsters of the Greek Myths*. New York: Bantam, 1975. Grades 4–8.

Fisher, Leonard Everett. *The Olympians: Great Gods and Goddesses of Ancient Greece*. New York: Holiday House, 1984. Grades 3–5.

Green, Roger L. *Tales of Greek Heroes*. New York, Penguin, 1974. Grades 4–8.

McCaughrean, Geraldine. *Greek Gods and Goddesses*. New York: Simon & Schuster, 1998. Grades 3–6.

Williams, Marcia. *Greek Myths for Young Children*. Cambridge, MA: Candlewick Press, 1992. Grades 2 and up (older students will enjoy the comic-strip style).

BOOKS FOR TEACHERS

Fitzgerald, Robert, trans. *The Odyssey*. New York: Doubleday & Company, Inc., 1961.

Hamilton, Edith. *Mythology: Timeless Tales of Gods and Heroes*. 1942. Reprint. New York: Warner Books, 1999.

Lattimore, Richmond, trans. *The Iliad of Homer*. Chicago: University of Chicago Press, 1951.

Melville, A. D., trans. *Metamorphoses*. New York: Oxford University Press, 1986.

Rearick, John. *Greek Myths: 8 Short Plays for the Classroom*. New York: Scholastic, 1997.

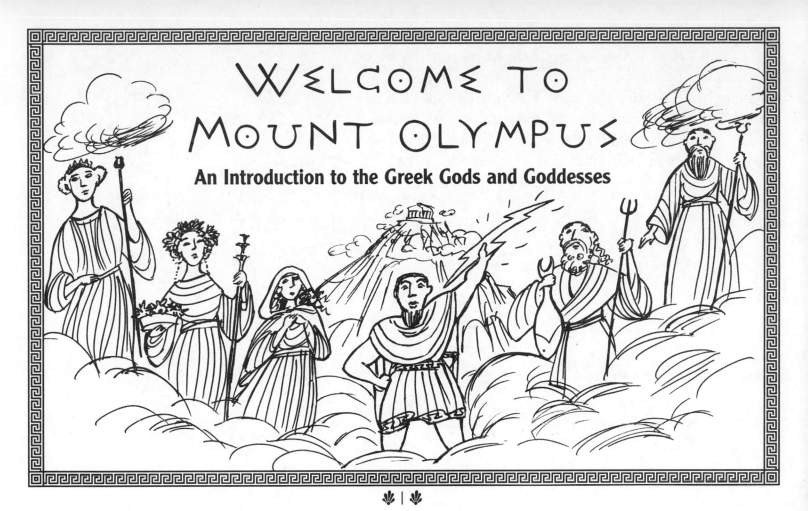

WELCOME TO MOUNT OLYMPUS

An Introduction to the Greek Gods and Goddesses

Uranus and Gaea fell in love and bore
12 mighty children, known as the Titans.
Cronos, the bravest of the bunch, decided
that Uranus had ruled long enough and
rose up against his father. Uranus fled,
realizing he was no match for his
powerful son.

Mount Olympus was no ordinary mountain. On this enormous and lofty mountain in ancient Greece, the trees grew taller, the grass grew greener, and the air smelled sweeter. The most unusual aspect of Mount Olympus was its inhabitants—the Greek gods and goddesses themselves. On this magical mountain, their story began with the first two deities: Gaea, the earth goddess, and Uranus, the sky god.

15 Greek Myth Mini-Books • Scholastic Professional Books

Cronos became the new ruler and married the goddess Rhea. As powerful as he was, Cronos was afraid of one thing: babies. He feared that one of his own children would overthrow him, just as he had overthrown his father. When Rhea gave birth to their first child, Cronos snatched the newborn baby and swallowed it whole.

After Cronos had swallowed their fifth child, Rhea came up with a plan. When their next child was born, Rhea named the baby Zeus and quickly hid him away. When Cronos demanded the newborn, she instead handed him a stone wrapped in a baby blanket. Cronos popped the stone in his mouth and gulped it down, blanket and all.

Rhea, will you bring me a glass of nectar to wash this down?

Of course, husband. Anything you say.

15 Greek Myth Mini-Books • Scholastic Professional Books

Meanwhile, young Zeus was happy and healthy, living in the care of nymphs on the outskirts of Mount Olympus. He grew into a strong and majestic god, and soon he yearned to live among the other deities.

⚜ 5 ⚜

The magic potion made Cronos so sick that he vomited up first the stone, then the blanket, and finally all five of his children— now fully grown gods and goddesses. Together with his brothers and sisters, Zeus battled his father and overthrew him.

⚜ 7 ⚜

Rhea missed her son terribly, so she brought him to Mount Olympus disguised as a royal servant. But this humble position did not satisfy the young god for long. One morning after Cronos did his daily exercises— a quick jog around the universe—he called for his new servant to fetch him a drink. Zeus quickly brought him a golden goblet, filled to the brim with a potion that he had mixed himself. Cronos slurped up the potion and then felt a terrible pain in his stomach.

Zeus now became the new ruler and chose Hera as his wife and queen. He then gave each of his siblings his or her own domain of power, so that he wouldn't have to look after everything himself. In time they would have help from their children and other divine relatives: Aphrodite, the goddess of love; Athena, the goddess of wisdom; Hermes, the messenger god; and many others. Yet even with the gods and goddesses in charge, things did not run as smoothly as one might think. There always seemed to be trouble brewing on Mount Olympus. . . .

15 Greek Myth Mini-Books • Scholastic Professional Books

JOURNEY TO THE UNDERWORLD

The Story of Persephone and Demeter

One day as Persephone was gathering flowers, she wandered away from her mother and lost all track of time. As she noticed Apollo's chariot setting lower in the sky, she turned toward home. Just then she spotted an unusual flower and bent to pick it. As she pulled up the flower, the earth suddenly split beneath her and a golden chariot emerged. The enormous driver wore a long black cape and a crown embedded with black gems. Before Persephone could scream for help, he pulled her into the chariot and they descended into the pit.

As goddess of the harvest, Demeter blessed the earth with all growing things. She loved the flowers, the trees, the fields, and all of her glorious creations, but most of all she loved her daughter, Persephone. Together they roamed about the earth, creating new kinds of plants, fruits, and flowers to suit their whims.

❦ 2 ❦

Demeter searched everywhere for her daughter, but days and weeks passed with no sign of Persephone. As Demeter grieved, the earth grew cold and barren. Leaves fell from the trees and nothing grew from the cracked, dry soil. The humans brought Demeter whatever sacrifices they could find—dead leaves and branches—hoping that the goddess would bless them with a harvest.

❦ 4 ❦

Demeter raced up Mount Olympus and demanded that Zeus return her daughter at once.

But sister, they are happily married. Persephone is queen of the Underworld and has a doting husband to look after her.

She will be miserable underground. Unless you return her to me, the earth will remain a wasteland and the humans will have nothing to offer you as a sacrifice.

Zeus knew that this would not do. He called for Hermes, the messenger god, to fetch Persephone and return her to Demeter.

But if she has eaten anything in the Underworld, even I cannot bring her back. It will be too late.

Zeus decided that he would make an exception, just this once. He ruled that for every pomegranate seed she ate, Persephone must spend one month in the Underworld with Hades. During these months, Demeter mourns the loss of her daughter and nothing grows on earth. Each year when Persephone returns to her mother, Demeter rejoices and everything on earth springs into full blossom. And so spring follows winter year after year, reflecting the moods of the harvest queen.

15 Greek Myth Mini-Books • Scholastic Professional Books

As Demeter continued to search, she came across a shepherd who had news of Persephone. He described what he had heard from another shepherd: Persephone had been kidnapped by a god driving a chariot pulled by four black horses. Demeter knew at once that the culprit was her own brother Hades, lord of the Underworld.

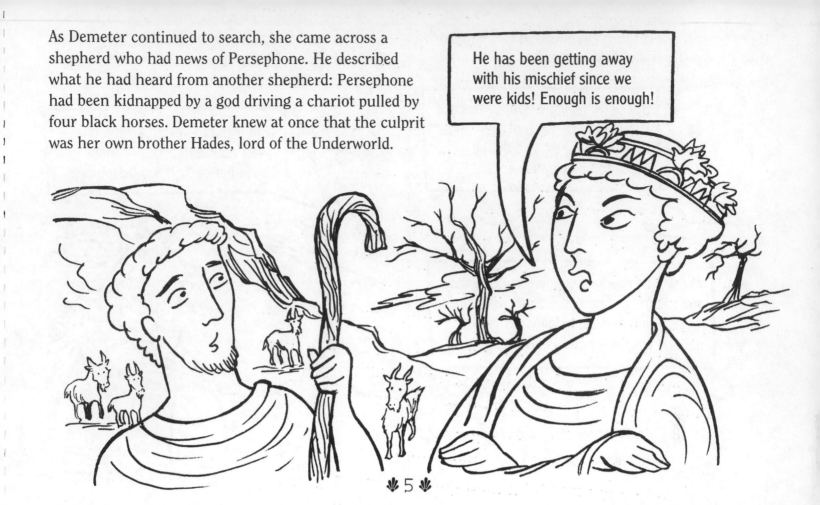

🌱 5 🌱

Persephone was overjoyed to see Hermes and learn that she would return to her mother. But when she heard the condition, she knew that all hope was lost. She had refused all of the tasty treats Hades had tempted her with, but just that morning she had eaten six tiny seeds from a pomegranate.

🌱 7 🌱

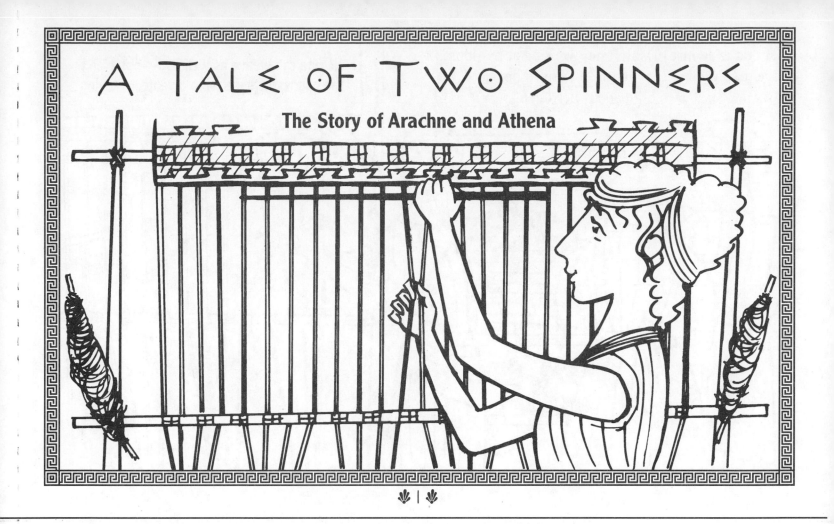

A Tale of Two Spinners

The Story of Arachne and Athena

Athena, the goddess of wisdom, thought she heard someone say her name. She swooped down from Mount Olympus to listen. When she heard the boastful girl daring to compare herself to a goddess, Athena disguised herself as an old woman and knocked on Arachne's door.

I hear that Athena has blessed you with great skill.

My talents are my own. Athena has nothing to do with it. She may be a goddess, but her skill is no match for mine.

Arachne was such a skilled weaver that people traveled far and wide just to watch her working at her loom. Eventually, all of the attention went to her head, and Arachne started to brag about her talent.

No one can weave as well as I—not even the goddess Athena, who invented weaving!

You may be a talented weaver, but you are a foolish girl. You should ask for Athena's forgiveness.

Forgive me? But I'm telling the truth! If Athena is insulted, she can pay me a visit. I'll be glad to show her a thing or two about weaving. We'd see who was the better weaver soon enough.

With that, Athena threw off her cloak and wig
and stood majestically before Arachne.

Well then, foolish girl, you're on.
Let the competition begin!

❧ 5 ❧

Athena was furious when she saw how Arachne had portrayed the
gods. She was even more outraged when she realized that her own
skill was only slightly better than the girl's. She shredded Arachne's
masterpiece and then struck her with the shuttle from her loom.

❧ 7 ❧

Crowds gathered to watch the weaving match. Never before or since have such creations flowed from the loom. Athena wove glorious scenes of the gods and goddesses, more beautiful and striking images than mortals had ever seen. Arachne also wove scenes of the gods, but she showed them as angry, jealous, and deceitful.

In that moment, Arachne began to shrink until her whole body was smaller than a little toe. She started to sprout legs until she had eight in all, and black hair grew all over her body. The tiny creature scurried to the highest spot it could find, and there it began weaving a delicate web—a home for the world's first spider.

CURIOSITY AND THE BOX

The Story of Pandora

He ordered Hephaestus to create a beautiful woman, and he named her Pandora. Aphrodite gave her the gift of beauty, Athena taught her various arts, and Zeus gave her a shiny golden box inlaid with precious stones and told her never to open it. Last, he gave her curiosity.

That's for me to know and you not to find out.

Why, thank you, Zeus. What's inside?

In the early days, life was very different for humans. It all changed, however, when they accepted the gift of fire from one of the less powerful gods, named Prometheus. Zeus was furious with the humans for not asking his permission first, so he devised a plan to punish them.

❧ 2 ❧

Hermes guided Pandora down from Mount Olympus and presented her to Prometheus's brother, Epimetheus. The two married and lived happily—except that Pandora could not forget about the forbidden box. Every night she lay awake thinking about what could be inside. She tied the box shut and locked it in a chest in the attic, but she could not get it out of her mind.

❧ 4 ❧

15 Greek Myth Mini-Books • Scholastic Professional Books

15 Greek Myth Mini-Books • Scholastic Professional Books

Pandora tried everything—stomping grapes, designing togas, playing the lyre—but nothing could get her mind off of that mysterious present. One night, Pandora lay awake, once again thinking about the little golden box.

The suspense is killing me! What's the harm in taking one little peek? Then I'll just close up the box and no one will ever know I opened it.

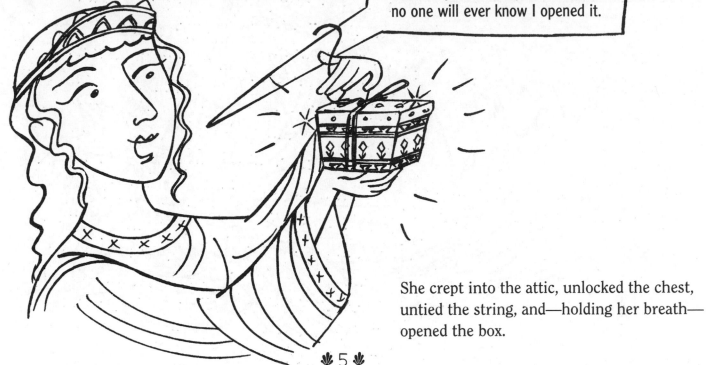

She crept into the attic, unlocked the chest, untied the string, and—holding her breath— opened the box.

❧ 5 ❧

Pandora shut the box as quickly as she could, trapping one last evil inside. This last evil was Despair— the total loss of hope.

❧ 7 ❧

Suddenly, a swarm of evils exploded from the small box, filling the air with howls of grief! Disease, Envy, Vanity, Spite, Old Age, Deceit, Distrust, and other miseries flew out of the box—evils that would plague humankind from that moment on.

If Despair had escaped from the box, people would never expect anything good to happen. All of their hopes and dreams would seem impossible, and they would simply give up. But with Despair trapped in the box, hope would survive. And hope is what keeps humankind optimistic, always looking at the bright side of what is yet to come.

Uh-oh. Now look at what I've done! But maybe this is just temporary. Surely I can catch these horrible things and put them back in their little box where they won't bother anyone. . . .

A Trip Around the World

The Story of Phaethon and Apollo

Clymene constantly reminded Phaethon that he was the son of powerful Apollo, and Phaethon reminded his friends of the fact every day at school. His friends soon grew tired of Phaethon's boasting.

Apollo this and Apollo that . . . you have an awful lot to say about someone you've never even met!

How do we even know he's your father in the first place? You look a bit scrawny to be the son of a god.

Although Clymene was a nymph in ancient Greece, she was not very different from mothers today. Clymene was extremely proud of her son Phaethon and knew that he was no ordinary young boy—especially since his father was no ordinary man. Phaethon's father was the sun god Apollo, who drove a fiery, golden chariot across the sky to bring light and warmth to the world.

❧ 2 ❧

Phaethon went home very upset that day. He couldn't help wondering if what his friends said was true. After all, he had never met Apollo. And the sun didn't shine any stronger on him than on anyone else.

I can't go back to school until I can prove that Apollo really is my father!

Well, you can pay him a visit tomorrow morning, while it is still dark outside. His palace is just a short distance to the east.

❧ 4 ❧

Excited and nervous, Phaethon set out on his short journey the next morning. He was glad he would finally meet his father, but he was also scared to come face to face with a god. Soon he reached a golden palace that seemed to glow, even though the sky was still dark. On shaky knees, Phaethon climbed the steep staircase and opened the enormous front door.

It was not difficult to find Apollo—all Phaethon had to do was follow the golden light. He shielded his eyes when he entered the throne room. Recognizing the young boy as his son, Apollo removed his glowing crown so that Phaethon could look directly at him.

At last you've decided to pay your old pop a visit. Come closer, Phaethon, so I can see how you've grown.

So it's true. You really are my father!

Please, Son, not that! You won't live to tell about it. I am the only one who can control those horses. Even Zeus himself could not do it.

But you said I could have whatever I wanted, and driving your chariot is the only thing I want.

Apollo tried to change Phaethon's mind, but the boy stubbornly refused. The chariot was due to light the sky in minutes, and Apollo was running out of time. He led Phaethon to the stables where the enormous golden horses were eager to set out on their daily journey. Placing Phaethon in the chariot, Apollo gave his best advice.

These horses are fast and powerful, unlike anything on earth. Hold tight to the reins and try to keep them on course. Don't let them veer too high, or the earth will freeze without the chariot's warmth. And don't drive too close to earth, or the chariot will burn everything with its heat.

On Mount Olympus, Zeus was roused from his sleep by screams of terror from the earth below. He was shocked to see Apollo's chariot swaying out of control—and a young boy in the driver's seat.

What was Apollo thinking, letting a minor drive his chariot—and a mortal, no less! I'll have a word with him later. There's only one thing to do now.

Apollo opened the stable doors and the horses burst into the sky. Within seconds, Phaethon lost his grip on the reins. Bewildered, the horses ran off course. First they bolted high into the sky, and then they plunged straight down toward the earth. They were close enough that Phaethon could see the destruction left in their path: Fields withered, oceans boiled, and mountains turned into volcanoes. The lands closest to the chariot baked and became the world's first deserts.

❧ 10 ❧

Zeus picked up a nearby lightning bolt and hurled it at the chariot. The lightning struck Phaethon and sent him flying from the chariot in a blaze of light. Those who saw it thought it was a shooting star falling from the sky into the ocean below. The horses returned to their stable, and the earth eventually recovered from its terror, but Apollo never forgave himself for making the foolish promise that cost his son's life.

❧ 12 ❧

15 Greek Myth Mini-Books • Scholastic Professional Books

GOSSIP AND VANITY

The Story of Echo and Narcissus

Echo continued to distract the powerful goddess with her endless prattle, while Zeus sneaked away from the scene. Hera turned around just in time to see her husband and realized that this impudent nymph was trying to trick her. In her fury, she punished Echo with a cruel curse: Echo would never be able to speak again, except to repeat the last words that others spoke to her.

If you lived on Mount Olympus and wanted to find out anything about anyone, you would ask Echo. She made it her business to mind everyone else's. One day, as Echo was eavesdropping on a friendly conversation between Zeus and a lovely nymph, she saw Zeus's wife, Hera, storming toward them. Before Hera could get a glimpse of Zeus, Echo grabbed her arm and began updating her on the latest gossip about the gods—leaving out Zeus, of course.

Echo wandered aimlessly through the woods, where she came upon Narcissus, the most beautiful young man ever to grace Mount Olympus. Echo caught one glimpse—that face, those eyes, that hair!—and instantly fell in love. She rushed to meet Narcissus, who was annoyed to be followed by yet another girl.

I don't want anything. Don't tell me you're another one of these foolish girls who think that they love me!

What do you want?

You want?

Love me!

No, I won't love you. I've yet to find anyone worthy of my love.

Meanwhile, Narcissus had stopped for a drink of water by a pool, where he saw the most beautiful face he had ever laid eyes on. And he finally discovered what it meant to be in love. But when Narcissus reached to touch the fair skin and golden locks, the face vanished beneath the ripples of water.

Come back! Don't leave me! Can't you see we're perfect for each other?

Narcissus turned to leave, and Echo was devastated. First she had lost her voice and now she was losing her heart to Narcissus. She hid herself in a cave and wept endlessly, until her body withered away and all that remained was her voice—an echo.

❦ ▷ ❦

When the water became still, the perfectly carved face reappeared. But every time Narcissus tried to touch it, the face disappeared in the waves. Narcissus vowed he would wait there forever for his beloved to come out. Little did he know that he had fallen in love with his own reflection. Narcissus waited day and night until a god took pity on him and changed him into a golden flower. And there he remained, a golden narcissus flower growing by the water.

❦ X ❦

MUSIC MAKES THE UNDERWORLD GO 'ROUND

The Story of Orpheus and Eurydice

The couple soon fell in love, and their wedding day was filled with music—the most joyful music Orpheus had ever played. But the happiness ended suddenly when Eurydice stepped on a poisonous snake as she was dancing and received a deadly bite.

The most beloved musician in all of Greece was Orpheus.
When he played his lyre and sang, all who heard him
forgot their troubles. Even animals would stop to listen,
and flowers and trees would turn to hear. His most
devoted fan of all was a young maiden named Eurydice.

❧ 2 ❧

Orpheus grieved for the loss of his wife, but he soon became tired
of feeling sorry for himself. He decided to travel to the Underworld
and bring Eurydice back with him. With his lyre, Orpheus set off.

First he came to the river Styx, where Charon takes spirits
across on his ferry. He asked to be carried across, but the stubborn
boatman refused. Orpheus began to play a song with the rhythm of
ocean waves, and even the hard-hearted Charon could not resist.

Can't you read the sign? . . .
Hades won't like this, but I'll
make an exception, just this once.

SPIRITS ONLY
beyond this point!

❧ 4 ❧

15 Greek Myth Mini-Books • Scholastic Professional Books

When he got off the ferry, Orpheus came face to face with a fierce three-headed dog. This was Cerberus, Hades' guard dog and beloved pet. Before the creature sank its three sets of fangs into his leg, Orpheus began to play a soothing song about lamb chops. The music lulled Cerberus to sleep, and soon all three of his mouths were drooling.

Orpheus continued playing songs as he made his way through the Underworld. The spirits who heard him forgot their surroundings and imagined they were alive and happy. Tantalus, who was punished with eternal thirst, forgot about drinking the forbidden water. Sisyphus forgot about the boulder he was doomed to push for eternity and let it slip and roll over his big toe.

❧ 5 ❧

Orpheus was overjoyed and set off at once. He played songs to distract himself, but he could not stop wondering if Eurydice was really following. What if Hades had tricked him into leaving the Underworld without his wife? After all, the gods were known to be cruel. If he left the Underworld, he might never get another chance to enter again—and all hope would be lost. As he neared the light of day, his fears grew stronger and he could not resist turning around for just one peek.

❧ 7 ❧

At last Orpheus came to Hades, seated beside Persephone, his queen. Orpheus begged to have his wife returned to him, but Hades would not hear of it. Then Orpheus played a song he had written about his loss, and even Hades could not help feeling the sadness of the music. Persephone took pity on Orpheus and whispered to her husband. Hades could not refuse her request to bend the rules, just this once.

As you are leaving the Underworld, Eurydice will follow behind you. But there is one condition: You must not look back. You must have faith that she is there.

There was his wife, just as happy as she looked on their wedding day. But as he reached out to grasp her hand, Eurydice vanished from sight.

15 Greek Myth Mini-Books • Scholastic Professional Books

CUPID FALLS IN LOVE

The Story of Cupid and Psyche

Psyche was annoyed by her trail of admirers. Meanwhile, Aphrodite, the goddess of love, watched Psyche and her devoted following from Mount Olympus. Like Psyche's sisters, Aphrodite grew jealous. The goddess of love called her son Cupid to help.

> Cupid, darling, shoot one of your arrows at that girl who is stealing all the attention. But make sure she falls in love with something ridiculous, like a pig or a goat!

Long, long ago, sisters did not always get along. Psyche and her two older sisters were no exception. Psyche's sisters were envious of her beauty and the number of suitors who followed her all over town.

What's so special about her?

15 Greek Myth Mini-Books • Scholastic Professional Books

Cupid had no choice but to obey his mother's orders, so he flew down to where Psyche lay sleeping. As he drew his bow and arrow, Cupid noticed how beautiful she was. He lost his concentration and accidentally scratched himself with the arrow. Not even the god of love can withstand the strength of his own arrows, and so Cupid fell in love for the very first time. From that moment on, Cupid guarded Psyche and made sure she never married.

Hey, what's happening to me? I suddenly feel light-headed and giddy!

15 Greek Myth Mini-Books • Scholastic Professional Books

Psyche's father consulted an oracle to learn why his daughter had not yet married. The oracle said that Psyche must be left on a mountainside to be claimed by her future husband. Fearful and alone, Psyche waited there until it grew dark. Suddenly, a gust of wind picked her up and carried her far away to a beautiful castle. She wandered inside and looked everywhere for her husband, terrified of whom or what she might find. But the castle was completely empty.

Psyche missed her husband during the long hours of the day. She grew so lonely that she asked if he could bring her sisters for a visit. The next day, the two sisters were whisked into the castle by a gust of wind. They marveled at the splendor of the palace and at Psyche's beautiful clothes, but jealousy gnawed at them.

Well, where is this famous husband who spoils you rotten with riches? Doesn't he have the manners to greet his wife's sisters?

Psyche made up an excuse, but finally broke down and told them that she had never actually seen her husband.

Never seen him? Then surely he is a hideous monster! Perhaps he is planning to gobble you up for dinner! You must take a peek at him while he is sleeping.

Psyche met her husband soon enough, but only at night when she could not see him. He was gentle and kind, and she grew to love him very much. But every day, as soon as Apollo's chariot began to light the sky, he fled the castle before she could catch a glimpse of him. When she asked him why this was so, he replied, "Trust me, my little valentine. I will let you see me in time."

❧ ▷ ❧

That night while her husband slept, Psyche lit an oil lamp and tiptoed to his side. She beheld the most beautiful sight—there, peacefully sleeping, lay the god of love. As she reached to touch his face, a drop of hot oil dripped from the lamp onto Cupid's shoulder and he awoke with a start. When he saw Psyche, he was heartbroken. He knew that she did not trust him, and that love can be built only upon trust. He flew out of the castle, never to return.

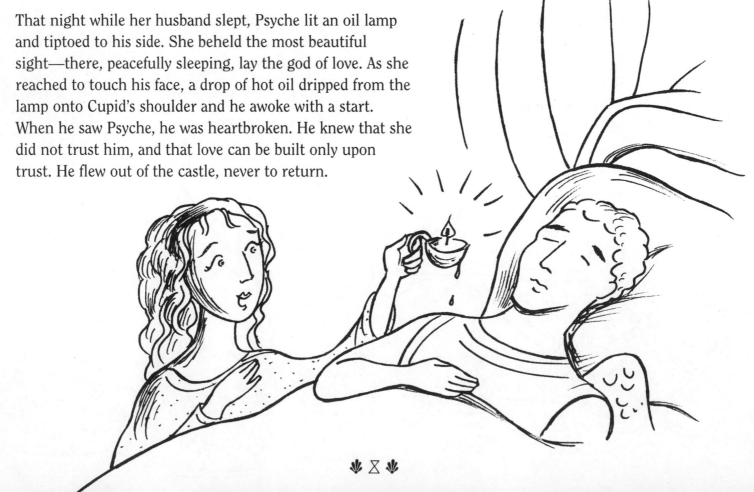

❧ X ❧

AN AMAZING BATTLE

The Story of Theseus and the Minotaur

King Aegeus protested at first, not wanting to risk his son's life.
But finally he gave in and made Theseus promise one thing.

On your trip home, replace the black sails with white sails as a sign that you are returning safely.

Every nine years, the cruel King Minos of Crete demanded that King Aegeus of Athens send him seven young men and seven young maidens. These young Athenians would be sacrificed to the Minotaur, a dreadful creature with the body of a man and the head of a bull. No one dared to oppose King Minos for fear that he would wage a terrible war in return. When the time came once again to choose the youths to be sacrificed, Theseus volunteered to go. Theseus was the brave and noble son of King Aegeus. His plan was not to be devoured by the Minotaur but to slay the beast once and for all.

15 Greek Myth Mini-Books • Scholastic Professional Books

When the Athenians arrived in Crete, they were welcomed by King Minos.

What a fine lot of Athenian men and women! A lovely snack for my pet Minotaur.

Snack! That's what you think.

And what makes you so bold?

The gods favor me.

15 Greek Myth Mini-Books • Scholastic Professional Books

To see if this was true, Minos gave Theseus an impossible task. He threw his blood-red ruby ring into the sea and ordered Theseus to fetch it. Theseus dove into the dark depths, praying to Poseidon for guidance. He swam deeper and deeper until he saw something glimmering in front of him. He grabbed the ring and sped back to the surface. Minos was furious, realizing that the gods most likely did favor this Athenian.

The next day, Theseus volunteered to be the first to face the Minotaur. As he entered the Labyrinth, he let the thread unwind behind him. Theseus made his way through the twists and turns of the maze until he reached its center, where he came upon a hideous snoring creature. Theseus crept up behind the bull-man and grabbed his horns—and a battle began. After a great struggle that lasted late into the night, Theseus managed to slay the beast.

Ariadne, the daughter of King Minos, watched as the Athenians were brought ashore to Crete. When she saw how proud and brave Theseus looked, even in chains, she instantly fell in love. That night she sneaked to his cell and whispered through the window.

Brave Athenian, you will not survive without my help. The Minotaur is kept in a Labyrinth, a maze of bushes that no one can find his way through. Please take this thread. Mark your path with it so that you can find your way out of the Labyrinth.

Thank you. What can I do for you in return?

Take me back to Athens with you. I am miserable here in Crete.

Theseus followed the thread to the entrance of the Labyrinth and quickly rounded up Ariadne and the prisoners. Since it was the middle of the night, no one saw them boarding their ship. But in their haste, Theseus forgot his promise to his father, and they set off with black sails instead of white.

Every day King Aegeus watched for signs of his son's return. One day as he stood watch, he noticed a ship on the horizon. As it drew nearer, Aegeus saw that the sails were black and, in despair, he stepped off the cliff into the sea below. Since then, the sea has been known by the name of the grief-stricken king—the Aegean Sea.

DANGEROUS HEIGHTS

The Story of Daedalus and Icarus

That night, Daedalus and his son Icarus were led to the center of the Labyrinth. The guard carried candles to light the way. Since the guard had a son about the same age as Icarus, he took pity on them and left some candles behind.

The famous inventor Daedalus spent many years working for King Minos. In fact, it was Daedalus who designed the maze of bushes where the Minotaur was kept. After Theseus killed the Minotaur and escaped from the Labyrinth, King Minos was furious with Daedalus.

How could he have escaped, Daedalus? As your punishment, you shall be imprisoned in the Labyrinth you created! And take that son of yours with you!

❧ 2 ❧

The next morning, Daedalus awoke to the sound of birds chirping. When he opened his eyes, he remembered with dismay where he was. He watched a bird gobble up a worm for breakfast and fly up and away from the Labyrinth.

I know! We'll fly out of here! I'll create wings for us. It's our only hope!

❧ 4 ❧

15 Greek Myth Mini-Books • Scholastic Professional Books

Daedalus and Icarus spent the next few days gathering all the feathers they could find. Then Daedalus fashioned two sets of wings by gluing the feathers together with hot candle wax.

Dad, are you done yet? How much longer?

You asked that five minutes ago. Have patience, Son.

❧ 5 ❧

Early the next morning they flew up and away, just like the birds. Daedalus looked back and all he could see of the Labyrinth was a tiny spot of green, getting smaller and smaller until it was gone. The sky was bright and beautiful, the air was cool, and the sun shone pleasantly on him. He began to relax and his eyelids grew heavy.

❧ 7 ❧

At last the wings were finished. The father and son put on their wings and practiced taking off and landing. Icarus could not wait to take to the sky.

Just remember, if you fly too low, the ocean water will splash your wings and weigh you down. And if you fly too high, the sun will melt the wax on your wings. You must follow me and stick to the middle course.

❀ ▷ ❀

Icarus flapped ahead of his father, excited to see everything the sky had to offer. He wanted to fly right through a fluffy white cloud, just to see what it felt like. He flew higher and higher, but the clouds were always above him, just out of reach. Determined, Icarus flapped even harder.

Sweat dripped from his forehead, and soon he felt something drip on his arm. It was the wax, melting from the sun's hot rays. Icarus called to his father for help, but Daedalus was too far behind. Feathers began to fall from his wings in clumps, and then Icarus himself began to fall—down, down, down—toward the sea below.

❀ X ❀

15 Greek Myth Mini-Books • Scholastic Professional Books

THE RACE FOR LOVE

The Story of Atalanta

Many years later in the nearby town of Calydon, everyone was in a panic. A wild boar was ravaging the land and no one could stop it. This was not an ordinary boar—it was sent by the goddess Artemis to punish the people for being so stingy with their sacrifices. The king of Calydon gathered all of the best hunters, including his son Meleager, to tackle the beast once and for all. They were ready to set out when an unusual hunter showed up—a woman!

Atalanta's father was not very pleased when she was born. He was a king who was used to getting what he wanted. He told his wife he wanted a son, and what did he get? A daughter. He was so disgusted that he ordered a servant to leave the infant on a mountainside to fend for herself. There, a family of bears found the girl and—thinking she resembled a baby bear without any fur—they adopted her.

❧ 2 ❧

The young woman, strangely dressed from head to toe in animal skins, looked confident and strong. This was Atalanta, the once-abandoned baby, who was now grown up and quite good at fending for herself. The bears had also taught her a thing or two about hunting. Meleager admired her courage and made sure she was allowed to join the hunting party.

❧ 4 ❧

15 Greek Myth Mini-Books • Scholastic Professional Books

The group found the boar soon enough—his enormous size made him easy to spot. But his speed, cunning, and ferocity made him almost impossible to conquer. The boar raced around the hunters, throwing them into confusion. Arrows zipped through the air, catching more hunters than anything else. Finally, an arrow hit the boar behind the ear, and it fell to the ground.

❧ 5 ❧

The horrible news soon reached Meleager's mother, Althaea. Outraged that her son had murdered her two brothers, Althaea raced to the highest tower of the castle and unlocked a small closet that held only a log. When Meleager was a baby, the Fates—three old women who have the power to decide the future—came to visit Althaea. They placed a log in the fire and said that Meleager would live as long as the log remained unburned. Althaea had pulled the log from the fire and safeguarded it from that day on. But now she took out the log and threw it into the hearth where a fire blazed.

❧ 7 ❧

Meleager finished the boar off with his sword and then offered the prized pelt and tusks to Atalanta.

If your arrow hadn't knocked the boar down, I wouldn't have been able to kill it.

But Meleager, since you killed the beast, the prize is yours!

A heated argument began, and Meleager's uncles said terrible things about Atalanta. Insults turned into pushes, pushes into punches, and—in his fury—Meleager killed his two uncles.

❧ ▷ ❧

At that moment, Meleager and Atalanta were gazing into each other's eyes. They were talking about their future together—marriage, children, and lots of hunting—when suddenly Meleager jumped up, ran circles around Atalanta, and collapsed at her feet. As the fire consumed the cursed log, it consumed Meleager's life as well. Atalanta vowed that she would never love again and never marry.

❧ ✕ ❧

15 Greek Myth Mini-Books • Scholastic Professional Books

After the boar hunt, everyone wanted to find out who this mysterious huntress was and where she had come from. The king who had once abandoned Atalanta now apologized and declared that he was proud of his daughter's bravery, strength, and skills. He wouldn't hear of Atalanta living with the bears any longer, and soon she was back in the castle.

When the suitors heard this, many of them gave up. They knew that Atalanta was faster than anyone—man or woman. But the rest were too love-struck to leave. They were willing to risk their lives for the small chance of winning Atalanta as their bride.

Now that she was a princess (and one whose bravery and skill won many admirers), Atalanta had suitors lining up outside the castle. But she would not even let them in the door—she had not forgotten her vow. The king was getting frustrated with his daughter's stubborn ways and had a word with her.

Atalanta, there are perfectly good potential husbands out there! Certainly one of them would meet your standards, if you would just give them a chance.

All right, Father. Let them race me. He who wins, wins my hand in marriage. He who loses, dies.

❧ 10 ❧

One young man knew it would take more than just luck to outrun Atalanta. Hippomenes prayed to the goddess of love for her help. Aphrodite was always in favor of setting up a good match, so she gave Hippomenes three delectable golden apples and told him the plan. He hid the apples in his tunic and prepared for the race.

❧ 12 ❧

15 Greek Myth Mini-Books • Scholastic Professional Books

Atalanta's father gave the signal, and the runners were off. They were neck and neck for the first few minutes, but soon Atalanta left Hippomenes in the dust. It was time to give Aphrodite's plan a try. Hippomenes pulled out one of the golden apples and threw it in Atalanta's direction, slightly out of her way.

What an unusual apple! I can afford a few seconds to pick it up.

13

Atalanta quickly caught up to him and dashed toward the finish line. Hippomenes took out the third and final apple—his only chance to win the race and save his life. Confident that she would win, as always, Atalanta thought nothing of stopping for one last apple. But Hippomenes had thrown the apple far off the track, and Atalanta misjudged how long it would take her to reach it. Hippomenes won the race by a few steps, and he also won the fastest bride in Greece.

15

Hippomenes caught up, but Atalanta again sped ahead.
Hippomenes threw the second apple farther off to the side.
Atalanta could not resist the second apple either, and she
darted after it. Hippomenes burst into the lead!

❧ 14 ❧

THE GOLDEN TOUCH

The Story of King Midas

Midas once did a favor for a god, and in return he was granted one wish—anything he wanted. Midas thought long and hard.

How could one wish satisfy his countless desires? He thought he deserved at least three. After all, weren't three wishes the standard reward? He felt cheated until an idea struck him like a flash.

> I know how I can get it all! My wish is that everything I touch will turn to gold!

King Midas was a greedy man—in fact, he was one of the greediest people who ever lived. All day long he thought about how much gold he had, and all night he dreamed about how he could get even more.

❧ 2 ❧

Midas could not resist testing his new power immediately. He reached out and broke off a twig from a tree. To his delight, the twig became solid gold. He began grabbing everything in sight—dirt, leaves, grass, flowers—and everything he touched hardened into pure gold.

I'll be the wealthiest, most powerful king in all the world! I'm going to spend every minute of the day turning things into gold. I won't even stop to sleep!

❧ 4 ❧

15 Greek Myth Mini-Books • Scholastic Professional Books

The greedy king worked up quite an appetite rushing about, tagging everything in sight. After many hours, he returned to the castle to order a royal feast. As he sat down, the table and chair turned to gold at his touch. He noticed with glee that the cup became a golden goblet in his hand. Midas took a sip of water to quench his terrible thirst and suddenly choked on a glob of metal! Spitting it out, he realized the water had turned to gold.

❧ 5 ❧

Sobbing, Midas collapsed on the floor and begged the gods for mercy. His tears fell like tiny golden marbles, which only made him cry harder.

I have learned my lesson! I was too greedy and am punished for it. Now I know that riches cannot buy happiness. Please take away all of this gold and let things return to the way they were!

❧ 7 ❧

Midas picked up a piece of bread and shoved it into his mouth as quickly as he could. But he could not outsmart his golden touch—as soon as the bread touched his lips, it turned into a chunk of gold.

> What is the use of having more gold than Apollo if I can't even eat a piece of bread? I'll be the richest, hungriest king in history!

Storming out of the banquet hall, Midas bumped into a servant. He turned to yell at the servant for getting in his way but instead came face to face with a life-sized golden statue.

❧ ▷ ❧

The gods took pity on the pathetic king and took away the Midas touch—which was, after all, a curse rather than a gift. But just in case Midas forgot his own foolishness, the gods gave him a reminder. Two donkey ears sprouted from the top of his head, and Midas never forgot his lesson.

❧ ⋈ ❧

15 Greek Myth Mini-Books • Scholastic Professional Books

CARVED TO PERFECTION
The Story of Pygmalion

Travelers came from far and wide to buy Pygmalion's masterpieces. Pygmalion wished he could keep all of his statues, but he needed to earn his living. He was always sorry to part with a statue—he felt as if each one held a little part of himself that he would never see again. As talented as Pygmalion was, he could never make the same statue twice. As he carved, each statue seemed to take on its own personality.

On the island of Cyprus lived a sculptor named Pygmalion. Every day, Pygmalion awoke before sunrise and carved statues until late in the evening. He chiseled and polished until the marble forms looked so lifelike that they seemed ready to spring from his hands.

Pygmalion spent all of his time by himself, except when people came to buy his work. Pygmalion didn't mind his solitary lifestyle. In fact, he preferred it because it allowed him to get more work done. But one night he had a strange dream that changed everything. Pygmalion dreamed that he met a woman who was more lovely, graceful, and kind than anyone he had ever known. He was so happy in his dream that when he awoke, Pygmalion felt lonely for the first time in his life.

15 Greek Myth Mini-Books • Scholastic Professional Books

He wondered about the woman in his dream. Did she exist? Would he ever meet her? Sadly, Pygmalion realized that even if she did exist, the chances were small that he would ever find her. When Pygmalion picked up his tools and began to carve, the image of the woman was still in his mind. As his hands chiseled, the face from his dream began to emerge from the marble.

Each year the people of Cyprus celebrated the feast of Aphrodite, the goddess of love. Pygmalion had never been interested in this particular feast, but this year he had an idea. Pygmalion traveled to the altar of Aphrodite and prayed that she would send him the woman from his dream, the woman whose image he had carved so perfectly.

Pygmalion carved for days on end, stopping only for a quick drink of water or a bite of food. When he finished, he collapsed with exhaustion and admired his work. There, standing before him, was the woman of his dreams. As Pygmalion gazed at the statue, he felt that she was gazing right back at him. So lifelike was the statue, it looked as though it would step off the pedestal at any moment.

Pygmalion named the statue Galatea and brought her presents. He slipped golden rings upon her fingers and draped pearls around her neck, but she did not smile as she had in his dream. He told her witty jokes, but she did not laugh. He played music for her, but she stood as still as ever. He sadly realized that he could love this statue with all his heart, but the statue could bring him no happiness. It would never love him in return.

❧ ▷ ❧

When Pygmalion returned from the feast, he held his breath and entered his home. The statue stood exactly where he had left it, as still and lifeless as ever. With a heavy heart, Pygmalion approached the statue and took her cold hand in his. He decided it would be best to part with the statue and leaned to kiss her hand good-bye.

At that moment, the marble hand became as soft and warm as his own. Pygmalion looked up and saw her cheeks flush with color, her lips curve into a smile, and her eyes shine with happiness—she was alive! Still holding her hand, Pygmalion helped Galatea step down from the pedestal. Aphrodite had heard his prayers and blessed the joyful couple as they embraced.

❧ Ⅹ ❧

A PETRIFYING QUEST

The Story of Perseus and Medusa

King Acrisius learned some very bad news when he consulted an oracle: His daughter Danae would bear a son who would kill him! Acrisius built a brass tower—with no doors and only a tiny slit for a window—and imprisoned his daughter inside. This prison, however, did not prevent Zeus from visiting Danae. He simply transformed himself into a ray of golden light and slipped through the narrow window. Since there was no way into or out of the tower, you can imagine how surprised Acrisius was when he heard a baby crying inside!

What's that I hear?
A baby?
It's impossible!

In ancient times, kings were always worrying about the future. Would they fall from power? And if so, who would replace them? To find out the answers to their questions, the kings consulted oracles. If they learned bad news, they foolishly thought maybe—just maybe—they could try to change their fates. But fate is fate, and even the most powerful kings could not change it.

15 Greek Myth Mini-Books • Scholastic Professional Books

Suspecting that the gods might be involved, Acrisius did not dare to harm the infant. Instead, he placed both Danae and her baby in a large wooden chest and pushed them off into the sea to fend for themselves. But the plan did not work as Acrisius intended. The chest floated smoothly through the ocean and soon landed safely on an island. The king of the island, named Polydectes, admired Danae and took both mother and son into his care.

There, there, baby Perseus, don't cry. Your father, Zeus, will make sure that we are safe and sound.

15 Greek Myth Mini-Books • Scholastic Professional Books

Years passed, and Perseus grew into a noble young man. Unfortunately, King Polydectes was less than noble. He had a sneaky plan to marry Danae and wanted to get her protective son out of the picture. Appealing to Perseus's sense of bravery and adventure, the king challenged Perseus to fetch the head of Medusa. Perseus accepted and asked the gods for help.

Perseus flew north until he reached a bleak, gloomy landscape that was scattered with unusual rocks. As he flew down for a closer look, he realized this was Medusa's territory. He could see that the strange-looking rocks had once been unlucky people who had looked in the wrong direction.

Since the gods favored Perseus, they equipped him for his quest.
Hermes, the messenger god, visited Perseus and brought him gifts:
winged sandals, a sickle-shaped sword, a shiny shield,
a helmet that would make Perseus invisible, and
some wise advice from Athena. With his new
gear, Perseus set off.

Following Athena's advice, Perseus
looked for Medusa in the reflection
of his shield. This way he would not
view her directly and could resist
her "petrifying" effect. Perseus soon
found Medusa fast asleep on a bed of
stones. He sneaked up quietly, but
Medusa's snake-hair awoke and
began hissing furiously. As Medusa
began to stir in her sleep, Perseus
raised his sword and swiftly chopped
off her head. Resisting the urge to
look, Perseus placed the still-hissing
head in a sack and headed home.

As he was flying home, Perseus spotted an unusual sight: a beautiful woman chained to a cliff beside the ocean. This was Andromeda, who was being sacrificed to a horrible sea monster in order to save her city. As he saw the monster emerge from the water, Perseus put on the invisibility helmet and swooped down for a fight. Perseus killed the monster with one slash of his sword and then took off the helmet to introduce himself to Andromeda. Surely this woman was destined to be his wife, he thought.

Perseus to the rescue! I wonder if this lovely lady is single.

❦ 9 ❦

And what ever happened to Acrisius, who was fated to die by Perseus's hand? Later in life, Perseus became a famous discus thrower, whom sports fans traveled far and wide to watch. At a tournament, Perseus accidentally threw a discus into the crowds where it hit and killed a spectator, none other than Acrisius. As hard as he had tried, Acrisius could not change his destiny.

❦ 11 ❦

Carrying Andromeda in his arms, Perseus arrived home just in time to halt the wedding that was planned for that day. Danae told Perseus how she was being forced to marry Polydectes. Perseus stormed to the castle and found him. Before Polydectes could get over his surprise at seeing Perseus still alive, Perseus pulled Medusa's head from the sack and held it right before the king's beady eyes.

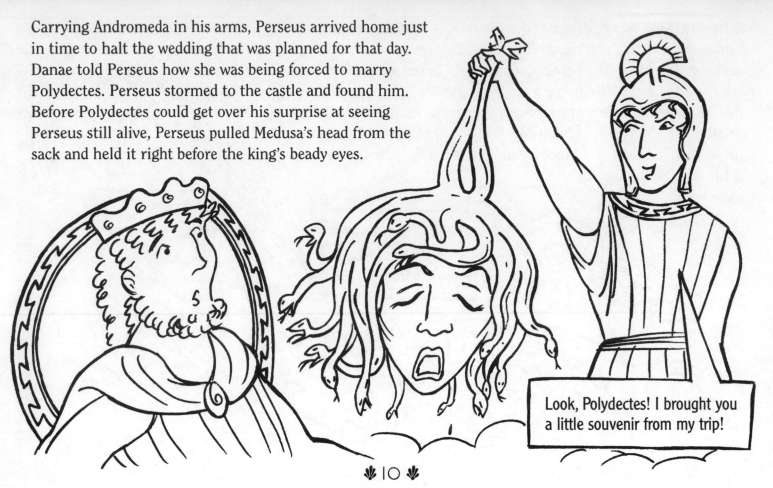

❦ 10 ❦

THE MYSTERIOUS HORSE

The Story of the Trojan War

Menelaus was not going to put up with this. He and the courageous leader Odysseus gathered forces in Greece, and they set out to bring Helen back. The Greeks landed on the beaches of Troy, and a war began that would last ten long years. After countless battles involving some of the bravest warriors of the time, and sometimes even the gods and goddesses, the Greeks never made it inside the city walls. The soldiers longed to return home, but Odysseus would not give up.

The most beautiful woman in ancient Greece was the cause of one of the most terrible wars. This great beauty was Helen, queen of Sparta and wife of Menelaus. But that didn't stop Paris from kidnapping her and bringing her to his home in Troy. The Trojans welcomed Helen to her new home, and soon she was known as Helen of Troy.

One morning, the Trojans were amazed to discover that the Greeks had gone home. The beaches were now deserted. Strangely enough, all that was left was an enormous wooden horse! The Trojans were puzzled by the strange horse and debated about what should be done with it.

Let's burn it. Those mischievous Greeks are probably up to one of their tricks!

Perhaps they built it as a gift to the gods so they would be granted a safe trip home.

Let's bring it inside the city. Maybe the gods will think we built it for them, and we'll be blessed instead.

The Trojans decided to bring the enormous, heavy horse inside the city walls for their victory celebration. The horse would serve as a pleasant reminder that the Greeks had surrendered to the mighty Trojans.

❦ 5 ❦

The Greeks opened the city gates and signaled to the rest of their army, who were on ships hidden behind an island. Soon the entire Greek army poured into Troy, without even one Trojan awake to stop them.

❦ 7 ❦

The joyful festivities lasted late into the night. When the last reveler had finally gone home to bed, a rumbling was heard in the horse's belly. A small door opened, and Greek soldiers popped out of the gigantic hollow horse! The Trojans had carried the Greeks right into the center of Troy—just as Odysseus had promised.

After a swift victory, Menelaus brought Helen back to her home in Sparta. Little did the Greeks know that some of them would not make it home for a long time. It would take Odysseus another ten years before he stepped foot in Greece. His return trip home, called the *Odyssey*, is a story unto itself.

GLOSSARY AND PRONUNCIATON GUIDE

Acrisius (a-KRIS-ee-us) Father of Danae; accidentally killed by his grandson, Perseus

Aegeus (ee-JEE-us) King of Athens; father of Theseus

Althaea (al-THEE-uh) Mother of Meleager; killed her son by placing a cursed log in the fire

Andromeda (an-DROM-eh-dah) Maiden rescued by Perseus from a sea monster

Aphrodite (af-reh-DI-tee) Goddess of love; Venus (Roman)

Apollo (uh-PAH-loh) Sun god; son of Zeus and Leto; twin of Artemis; Sol, Hyperion, Phoebus, Helios (Roman)

Arachne (uh-RACK-nee) Young woman who competed in a weaving contest with Athena; turned into a spider by Athena

Ariadne (ar-ee-AD-nee) Daughter of King Minos; gave Theseus thread to help him escape from the Labyrinth

Artemis (AR-tuh-mis) Moon goddess and goddess of the hunt; daughter of Zeus and Leto; twin of Apollo; Diana (Roman)

Atalanta (at-uh-LAN-tuh) Huntress who helped Meleager slay the Calydonian boar; married Hippomenes after he outran her in a footrace

Athena (uh-THEE-nuh) Goddess of wisdom; turned Arachne into a spider; Minerva (Roman)

Cerberus (SER-ber-us) Three-headed guard dog of the Underworld

Charon (KAR-on) Boatman who carried souls to the Underworld

Clymene (KLIM-eh-nee) Nymph; mother of Phaethon

Cronos (CROH-nus) A Titan; son of Gaea and Uranus; husband of Rhea; swallowed his children so they would not depose him; Saturn (Roman)

Cupid (KEW-pid) God of love; son of Aprhodite; fell in love with Psyche; also called Eros

Daedalus (DED-uh-lus) Inventor; father of Icarus; designed the Labyrinth and was imprisoned in it by King Minos; escaped by building wings

Danae (DAN-ay-ee) Mother of Perseus; daughter of Acrisius; imprisoned in a tower and visited by Zeus

Demeter (dee-MEE-tuhr) Goddess of the harvest; mother of Persephone; Ceres (Roman)

Echo (ECK-oh) Nymph and gossip; punished by Hera to repeat the last words of others; fell in love with Narcissus

Epimetheus (ep-uh-MEE-thee-us) Husband of Pandora; brother of Prometheus

Eurydice (yu-RID-uh-see) Wife of Orpheus; died on her wedding day and was almost rescued from the Underworld by Orpheus

Gaea (JEE-uh) Earth goddess; wife of Uranus; mother of Cronos and the other Titans

Galatea (gal-uh-TEE-uh) Statue carved by Pygmalion and brought to life by Aphrodite

Hades (HAY-deez) God of the Underworld; kidnapped and married Persephone; Pluto (Roman)

Helen (HEL-en) Queen of Sparta; beautiful wife of Menelaus; brought to Troy by Paris, starting the Trojan War

Hephaestus (heh-FEHS-tus) God of fire; son of Zeus and Hera; married to Aphrodite; Vulcan (Roman)

Hera (HEER-uh) Wife of Zeus; goddess of women and motherhood; Juno (Roman)

Hermes (HER-meez) Messenger god; son of Zeus; Mercury (Roman)

Hestia (HES-tee-uh) Goddess of the hearth and home; Vesta (Roman)

Hippomenes (hip-AHM-ih-neez) Suitor of Atalanta; won Atalanta's hand in marriage by winning a footrace

Icarus (IK-uh-rus) Son of Daedalus; escaped from the Labyrinth but fell into the sea when his wings melted

Medusa (meh-DOO-sah) Snake-haired Gorgon who turned onlookers to stone; slain by Perseus

Meleager (mel-ee-AY-juhr) Hunter of Calydonian boar; suitor of Atalanta; died when his mother placed a cursed log in the fire

Menelaus (men-uh-LAY-us) King of Sparta; husband of Helen; fought in the Trojan War

Midas (MY-das) Greedy king who could turn everything he touched to gold

Minos (MY-nahs) King of Crete; father of Ariadne; demanded Athenians to feed to the Minotaur; imprisoned Daedalus and Icarus in the Labyrinth

Minotaur (MIH-nuh-tor) Creature with the head of a bull and the body of a man; kept in the Labyrinth by Minos; slain by Theseus

Narcissus (nar-SIS-us) Beautiful and vain youth who fell in love with his own reflection

Odysseus (oh-DIS-ee-us) Wise Greek leader during the Trojan War; Ulysses (Roman)

Oeneus (EE-nee-us) King of Calydon; father of Meleager

Orpheus (OR-fee-us) Musician; attempted to rescue his wife, Eurydice, from the Underworld

Pandora (pan-DOR-ah) First mortal female; wife of Epimetheus; opened a box and released evils to plague humankind

Paris (PAR-is) Prince of Troy; kidnapped Helen and brought her to Troy, starting the Trojan War

Persephone (per-SEF-uh-nee) Daughter of Demeter; kidnapped by Hades and brought to the Underworld; Proserpine or Proserpina (Roman)

Perseus (PUR-see-us) Son of Zeus and Danae; grandson of King Acrisius; beheaded Medusa; rescued and married Andromeda

Phaethon (FAY-uh-thun) Son of Apollo and Clymene; drove Apollo's chariot off course and was killed by Zeus

Polydectes (pol-uh-DEK-teez) King who attempted to marry Danae; turned to stone by Perseus

Poseidon (poh-SY-duhn) God of the sea; Neptune (Roman)

Prometheus (pro-MEE-thee-us) God who disobeyed Zeus by giving fire to humans; punished by having his liver pecked by an eagle

Psyche (SY-key) Wife of Cupid; disobeyed Cupid by looking at him while he slept

Pygmalion (pig-MAIL-yun) Sculptor who fell in love with his statue, Galatea

Rhea (REE-uh) Wife of Cronos; mother of Zeus

Sisyphus (SIS-uh-fus) Man condemned in the Underworld to push a boulder uphill for eternity

Tantalus (TAN-tuh-lus) Man punished in the Underworld with eternal hunger and thirst

Theseus (THEE-see-us) Son of Aegeus; slew the Minotaur

Uranus (yoo-RAY-nus) The first and oldest god; god of the sky; husband of Gaea; father of Cronos and the other Titans; overthrown by Cronos

Zeus (ZOOS) Son of Cronos and Rhea; overthrew Cronos to become the ruler of heaven and earth; husband of Hera; Jove or Jupiter (Roman)